I0620195

Flow

Transform Your Life with the Power of Positive Energy:
Master the Art of Living in the Moment and Unlock Your
Full Potential with the Principles of Flow

Lance P. Richards

Flow: Transform Your Life with the Power of Positive Energy: Master the Art of Living in the Moment and Unlock Your Full Potential with the Principles of Flow

Table of Contents

01: Introduction to the Concept of Flow

The concept of flow is one that has been gaining popularity in recent years, as more and more people are recognizing the transformative power it can have on their lives. But what exactly is flow, and why is it so important? In this chapter, we will explore the origins of flow and its key components, so that you can better understand what it is and how it can be used to enhance your life.

Flow is a state of being that is characterized by a deep sense of focus, engagement, and enjoyment. It is a feeling of being completely absorbed in the moment, of doing something you love and finding it effortless and satisfying. Flow is often described as the feeling of being in the zone, where you are completely in sync with your surroundings and have a heightened sense of awareness and control over your thoughts and actions.

The concept of flow was first introduced by psychologist Mihaly Csikszentmihalyi in the 1970s, and since then it has been the subject of extensive research and study. Csikszentmihalyi found that people who were in flow experienced a higher sense of well-being, creativity, and fulfillment than those who were not. He also discovered that flow was not limited to a particular type of activity or person, and that it could be experienced in a variety of settings, from work to leisure to sports.

Flow is often associated with optimal performance, as people who are in flow are able to access a higher level of cognitive and physical ability. However, flow is not just about performance; it is also about the experience of being fully engaged in what you are doing, of finding meaning and purpose in your actions. When you are in flow, you are not thinking about the future or the past; you are fully present in the moment, and that is what makes it such a powerful and transformative experience.

So what exactly makes flow such a powerful state of being? There are several key components to flow that make it so special, including:

– Complete focus and engagement: When you are in flow, you are fully focused on the task at hand, and you are completely absorbed in the moment. You are not distracted by external factors, and your mind is clear and focused.

– A sense of effortlessness: Despite the intense focus and

engagement, flow is characterized by a sense of effortlessness. You are not working hard to achieve your goals; you are simply doing what comes naturally to you, and it feels satisfying and enjoyable.

– A sense of control: When you are in flow, you have a heightened sense of control over your thoughts and actions. You know exactly what you need to do, and you have the skills and abilities to do it.

– A sense of fulfillment: Flow is not just about the experience of being in the moment; it is also about the sense of fulfillment that comes from doing something you love. When you are in flow, you are living your life to the fullest, and you feel a deep sense of purpose and meaning.

The benefits of flow are not limited to just one aspect of life. Whether you are at work, at home, or in any other setting, flow can enhance your overall sense of well-being and happiness. By learning how to cultivate flow in your life, you can tap into your full potential and experience the power of positive energy and living in the moment.

In conclusion, flow is a powerful and transformative state of being that can bring new levels of focus, engagement, and fulfillment to your life. By understanding the key components of flow, you can start to tap into its power and experience the full benefits for yourself. In the coming

02: Understanding the Power of Positive Energy

The power of positive energy is a concept that has been studied and explored by many thinkers, researchers, and spiritual leaders for centuries. It is a force that has the ability to transform your life, bringing new levels of happiness, joy, and fulfillment to your daily existence. But what exactly is positive energy, and how does it work? In this chapter, we will delve into the science and spirituality behind positive energy, so that you can better understand its impact on your life.

Positive energy is an intangible force that can be felt and experienced, but it cannot be seen or touched. It is the energy that is created when you have positive thoughts, feelings, and emotions, and it is this energy that has the power to transform your life. Positive energy is often associated with a sense of happiness, joy, and well-being, and it is this energy that attracts more positive experiences and opportunities into your life.

The science behind positive energy is rooted in the field of quantum physics, which has shown that everything in the universe is made up of energy. This energy is in constant

motion and it has the ability to change and transform. Positive energy is the energy of life, and it is the force that
drives all of creation.

One of the key principles of positive energy is the law of at-
traction, which states that like attracts like. This means that
the positive energy you put out into the world will attract
more positive energy back to you. If you are filled with positive thoughts, feelings, and emotions, then you will attract
more positive experiences and opportunities into your life.
Conversely, if you are filled with negative energy, you will
attract negative experiences and challenges.

The power of positive energy is not limited to just your
thoughts and feelings. It also extends to your actions and
behaviors. When you engage in positive behaviors and
activities, you are sending positive energy out into the
world, and this will have a positive impact on your life.
Whether you are volunteering, helping someone in need, or
simply smiling at a stranger, you are spreading positive energy and making a positive impact on the world.

One of the most important things to understand about positive energy is that it is contagious. When you are filled with

positive energy, you have the ability to spread it to others, and this can have a powerful impact on those around you. Whether you are at work, at home, or in any other setting, your positive energy can help to uplift and inspire those around you, and this can create a ripple effect of positive change.

The power of positive energy is not limited to just the physical world. It also has a spiritual aspect, and many spiritual leaders and traditions have recognized the importance of positive energy for centuries. Whether you believe in the power of prayer, meditation, or other spiritual practices, the principle remains the same: by focusing on positive energy, you can transform your life and bring new levels of happiness, joy, and fulfillment to your daily existence.

In conclusion, positive energy is a powerful force that has the ability to transform your life, bringing new levels of happiness, joy, and fulfillment to your daily existence. Whether you understand it from a scientific or spiritual perspective, the principles are the same: by focusing on positive energy and spreading it to those around you, you can make a positive impact on the world and experience the full benefits for yourself. In the coming chapters, we will explore different techniques and practices that can help you tap into the power of positive energy and transform your life.

03: The Benefits of Living in the Moment

Living in the moment is a concept that has been talked about and practiced for centuries, but it is only in recent years that it has gained mainstream popularity. The idea of being fully present and engaged in the here and now has been shown to have a range of benefits for mental, emotional, and physical well-being. In this chapter, we will explore the benefits of living in the moment, so that you can understand why this simple practice can have such a profound impact on your life.

The first benefit of living in the moment is that it can help to reduce stress and anxiety. When you are fully present and engaged in the here and now, you are not worrying about the future or dwelling on the past. Instead, you are focused on the present moment, and this can help to reduce stress and anxiety levels, bringing new levels of peace and calm to your daily existence.

Living in the moment can also help to improve your relationships. When you are fully present and engaged with the people around you, you are able to connect with them on a deeper level, and this can help to build stronger and more meaningful relationships. Whether you are spending time with family, friends, or coworkers, living in the moment can help you to build more meaningful and lasting connections with the people in your life.

Another benefit of living in the moment is that it can help to increase your creativity and productivity. When you are fully present and engaged in the here and now, your mind is clear and focused, and this can help you to tap into your innate creativity and productivity. Whether you are working on a project, problem-solving, or simply exploring new ideas, living in the moment can help you to be more productive and creative in all areas of your life.

Living in the moment can also help to improve your physical health. When you are fully present and engaged in the here and now, you are more likely to make healthier choices, such as eating well, getting regular exercise, and getting enough rest. Living in the moment can also help you to be more mindful of your body and its needs, so that you can make better decisions about your health and well-being.

Finally, living in the moment can help to bring more joy and happiness into your life. When you are fully present and engaged in the here and now, you are able to appreciate the small things in life, and this can help to bring new levels of joy and happiness to your daily existence. Whether you are enjoying a sunset, playing with your children, or simply taking a walk in nature, living in the moment can help you to appreciate the beauty and wonder of life in a new way.

In conclusion, living in the moment has a range of benefits for mental, emotional, and physical well-being. Whether you are looking to reduce stress and anxiety, improve your relationships, increase your creativity and productivity, or simply bring more joy and happiness into your life, living in the moment is a simple and effective practice that can have a profound impact on your life. In the coming chapters, we will explore different techniques and practices that can help you to live in the moment and unlock the full benefits for yourself.

04: The Science Behind Flow

Flow is a concept that has been studied by psychologists and researchers for decades, and the results of this research have provided valuable insights into the science behind this elusive state of being. In this chapter, we will explore the science behind flow, so that you can understand the mechanisms that make this state so powerful and transformative.

The first aspect of the science behind flow is the relationship between challenge and skill. Flow is achieved when a person is engaged in a task that is both challenging and within their skill level. This means that the task is difficult enough to be engaging, but not so difficult that it is frustrating or overwhelming. When this balance is achieved, the person enters a state of flow, in which they are fully absorbed and engaged in the task at hand.

Another aspect of the science behind flow is the role of feedback. In a state of flow, the person is receiving immediate and accurate feedback about their performance, which helps them to stay engaged and focused on the task. This feedback helps to create a sense of mastery and control, which is one of the key elements of flow.

The third aspect of the science behind flow is the role of focus. In a state of flow, a person's attention is fully focused on the task at hand, and this focus helps to create a sense of immersion and connection to the task. This focus helps to reduce distractions and increase the person's ability to perform at their best.

The fourth aspect of the science behind flow is the role of intrinsic motivation. In a state of flow, a person is driven by their own internal motivation and desire to complete the task, rather than external rewards or incentives. This intrinsic motivation helps to create a sense of purpose and meaning, which is another key element of flow.

Finally, the science behind flow also highlights the role of emotions in the flow experience. Research has shown that people who are in a state of flow experience positive emotions such as joy, excitement, and fulfillment, which further contribute to the sense of well-being and satisfaction that comes with flow.

In conclusion, the science behind flow provides valuable insights into the mechanisms that make this state so powerful and transformative. By understanding the relationship between challenge and skill, the role of feedback, focus, intrinsic motivation, and emotions, we can better understand the science behind flow and how it can be used to improve our lives and unlock our full potential. In the coming chapters, we will explore different techniques and practices that can help you to enter a state of flow and tap into its powerful benefits.

05: The Key Components of Flow

In the previous chapter, we explored the science behind flow, and now it is time to delve deeper into the key components of this elusive state. Understanding the key components of flow is crucial if you want to master the art of living in the moment and unlock your full potential with the principles of flow. In this chapter, we will explore each of the key components in detail, so that you can understand the essential elements of flow and how they interact to create this transformative state.

The first key component of flow is challenge and skill. As we discussed earlier, flow is achieved when a person is engaged in a task that is both challenging and within their skill level. This balance between challenge and skill creates a sense of engagement and focus, which is crucial for flow to occur. It is important to note that the challenge and skill level must be in balance, as too much challenge can lead to frustration, while too little challenge can lead to boredom.

The second key component of flow is focus. In a state of flow, a person's attention is fully focused on the task at hand, and this focus helps to create a sense of immersion and connection to the task. Focus is crucial for flow, as it helps to reduce distractions and increase the person's ability to perform at their best. Focus also helps to create a sense of clarity and concentration, which are essential for flow to occur.

The third key component of flow is feedback. Feedback is a critical aspect of flow, as it helps to create a sense of mastery and control. In a state of flow, the person is receiving immediate and accurate feedback about their performance, which helps them to stay engaged and focused on the task. Feedback is also essential for self-reflection and improvement, as it provides the person with information about their strengths and weaknesses, which can be used to make adjustments and improvements.

The fourth key component of flow is intrinsic motivation. Intrinsic motivation is the drive to engage in a task for the inherent satisfaction and enjoyment that comes from doing it, rather than for external rewards or incentives. In a state of flow, the person is driven by their own internal motivation and desire to complete the task, which helps to create a sense of purpose and meaning. Intrinsic motivation is a key component of flow, as it helps to sustain the person's focus and engagement throughout the task.

05: THE KEY COMPONENTS OF FLOW

The fifth and final key component of flow is positive emotion. In a state of flow, people experience positive emotions such as joy, excitement, and fulfillment, which contribute to the sense of well-being and satisfaction that comes with flow. Positive emotions are essential for flow, as they help to increase the person's motivation, energy, and engagement, and they also help to reinforce the flow state and make it more likely to occur in the future.

In conclusion, the key components of flow are challenge and skill, focus, feedback, intrinsic motivation, and positive emotion. Understanding these components is crucial if you want to master the art of living in the moment and tap into the power of positive energy. In the coming chapters, we will explore specific techniques and practices that can help you to cultivate each of these components, so that you can enter a state of flow and unlock your full potential.

06: Understanding Your Limits and Overcoming Them

In the previous chapter, we explored the key components of flow, and now it is time to take a closer look at the concept of limits. Limits are an integral part of our lives, and they can either facilitate or hinder our ability to achieve flow. In this chapter, we will examine the concept of limits, understand how they impact our ability to enter a state of flow, and explore practical strategies for overcoming them.

First, it is important to understand what limits are and how they impact our lives. Limits are essentially boundaries that we set for ourselves, based on our experiences, beliefs, and habits. These limits can take many forms, such as physical, emotional, mental, and spiritual boundaries, and they can impact our ability to achieve flow in a variety of ways. For example, limiting beliefs about our abilities, habits of negative self-talk, and lack of self-confidence can all serve as barriers to entering a state of flow.

In order to overcome our limits and enter a state of flow, it is important to understand the nature of these limits and how they impact our lives. This requires a deep level of self-awareness and introspection, as well as a willingness to examine our beliefs, attitudes, and habits. In order to gain this level of self-awareness, you can use tools such as journaling, meditation, and self-reflection to gain a deeper understanding of your limits and how they impact your ability to achieve flow.

Once you have a better understanding of your limits, it is time to start taking action to overcome them. There are several strategies that you can use to overcome your limits and enter a state of flow.

One effective strategy is to challenge your limiting beliefs. Limiting beliefs can hold us back from achieving our full potential, and they can be a major barrier to entering a state of flow. By challenging these beliefs and replacing them with more empowering ones, you can increase your ability to enter a state of flow. This can be done through visualization, affirmations, and other techniques that help to change your mindset and beliefs about yourself and your abilities.

Another strategy for overcoming limits is to increase your self-confidence. Self-confidence is a key factor in achieving flow, as it allows you to take risks and engage in challenging tasks with a sense of courage and determination. To increase your self-confidence, you can practice positive self-talk, set achievable goals, and seek out opportunities for growth and development.

A third strategy for overcoming limits is to cultivate a growth mindset. A growth mindset is the belief that you can continue to grow, develop, and improve throughout your life, regardless of your current abilities or circumstances. This type of mindset helps to create a sense of purpose and meaning, and it encourages you to take on new challenges and engage in tasks that are outside of your comfort zone. To cultivate a growth mindset, you can focus on learning new skills, embracing failure as a learning opportunity, and seeking out new experiences and challenges.

In conclusion, understanding your limits and overcoming them is an essential part of mastering the art of living in the moment and tapping into the power of positive energy. By gaining a deeper understanding of your limits and using practical strategies to overcome them, you can increase your ability to enter a state of flow and unlock your full potential. In the next chapter, we will explore specific techniques and practices that can help you to cultivate a positive and growth-focused mindset, so that you can achieve flow and transform your life.

07: Harnessing the Power of Your Mind

The mind is a powerful tool, and it has the ability to shape our perceptions, beliefs, and actions in ways that can either enhance or limit our ability to achieve flow. In this chapter, we will explore the ways in which the mind can impact our ability to live in the moment and harness the power of positive energy. We will also discuss specific techniques and practices that you can use to harness the power of your mind and achieve a greater sense of flow in your daily life.

One of the key ways in which the mind impacts our ability to achieve flow is through the power of perception. Our perceptions of the world around us are shaped by our beliefs, attitudes, and experiences, and they can have a profound impact on our ability to live in the moment and achieve flow. For example, if we hold negative beliefs about ourselves or the world, we may be more likely to experience feelings of anxiety, stress, and frustration, which can prevent us from entering a state of flow.

To harness the power of your mind and achieve flow, it is important to develop a positive and growth-focused mindset. This requires a deep level of self-awareness and introspection, as well as a willingness to examine your beliefs and attitudes and make changes where necessary. You can cultivate a positive and growth-focused mindset through a variety of techniques, such as affirmations, visualization, and meditation.

In addition to shaping our perceptions, the mind also has the ability to impact our thoughts and emotions. Our thoughts and emotions play a key role in determining our level of happiness, fulfillment, and well-being, and they can also impact our ability to achieve flow. For example, if we are constantly consumed by negative thoughts and emotions, such as anxiety, anger, and frustration, we may be less likely to enter a state of flow.

To harness the power of your mind and achieve flow, it is important to cultivate a sense of mental and emotional balance. This can be achieved through a variety of techniques, such as mindfulness, visualization, and positive self-talk. Mindfulness, for example, involves paying attention to the present moment and becoming more aware of your thoughts, emotions, and sensations. By practicing mindfulness, you can learn to respond to negative thoughts and emotions in a more positive and productive way, which can help you to achieve a greater sense of flow in your life.

Another way to harness the power of your mind and achieve flow is through visualization. Visualization involves using your imagination to create vivid, positive images of your desired outcomes. By visualizing yourself achieving your goals and experiencing positive emotions, you can increase your motivation, focus, and self-confidence, which can all help you to achieve flow.

Finally, to harness the power of your mind and achieve flow, it is important to cultivate a sense of purpose and meaning. Having a clear sense of purpose and direction in life can help you to stay focused, motivated, and energized, and it can also help you to achieve a greater sense of flow. To cultivate a sense of purpose and meaning, you can set achievable goals, engage in activities that align with your values and passions, and focus on making a positive impact in the world.

In conclusion, harnessing the power of your mind is an essential part of achieving flow and transforming your life. By developing a positive and growth-focused mindset, cultivating mental and emotional balance, visualizing your desired outcomes, and focusing on your purpose and meaning, you can harness the power of your mind and achieve a greater sense of flow in your life. In the next chapter, we will explore the role that physical activity and exercise play in achieving flow and unlocking your full potential.

08: The Importance of Mindfulness in Flow

Mindfulness is a concept that has gained immense popularity in recent years, and for good reason. Mindfulness refers to the practice of paying attention to the present moment, without judgment or distraction. It involves becoming more aware of your thoughts, emotions, and sensations, and learning to respond to them in a more positive and productive way. Mindfulness is an essential component of flow, as it helps to cultivate a sense of mental and emotional balance and focus, and can greatly enhance your ability to live in the moment and harness the power of positive energy.

One of the key benefits of mindfulness is that it helps to reduce stress and anxiety. In today's fast-paced world, stress and anxiety are all too common, and they can prevent us from achieving flow and living our best lives. By practicing mindfulness, you can learn to respond to stressful situations in a more positive and effective way, reducing feelings of anxiety and increasing your sense of peace and calm. This can be especially helpful in high-pressure or challenging situations, such as work or family responsibilities, as it can help you to remain centered and focused, even in the face of adversity.

Another benefit of mindfulness is that it helps to increase self-awareness. When we are mindful, we become more aware of our thoughts, emotions, and behaviors, which can help us to identify patterns of thought and behavior that may be holding us back from achieving flow. This increased self-awareness can help us to make positive changes in our lives, such as letting go of negative beliefs or habits that may be preventing us from living in the moment and experiencing flow.

Mindfulness can also help to increase our level of focus and concentration. In today's world, distractions are everywhere, and it can be easy to get sidetracked and lose focus. By practicing mindfulness, you can learn to focus your attention on the present moment and become more resilient to distractions. This increased focus and concentration can help you to achieve flow more easily, as it allows you to be fully present and engaged in the moment, without being sidetracked by external distractions.

Mindfulness can also help to improve our relationships with others. When we are mindful, we become more aware of our thoughts and emotions, and we learn to respond to others in a more positive and compassionate way. This increased emotional intelligence can help us to form deeper and more meaningful relationships, which can greatly enhance our overall well-being and happiness.

Finally, mindfulness can help to increase our sense of gratitude and appreciation. When we are mindful, we become more aware of the positive aspects of our lives, and we learn to appreciate the simple things that bring us joy and fulfillment. This increased sense of gratitude and appreciation can help us to experience more positive emotions, which can greatly enhance our ability to achieve flow.

In conclusion, mindfulness is a critical component of flow, and it offers a wide range of benefits that can help you to live in the moment, reduce stress and anxiety, increase self-awareness, improve focus and concentration, improve relationships, and increase your sense of gratitude and appreciation. By incorporating mindfulness into your daily routine, you can take your first step towards achieving flow and unlocking your full potential. In the next chapter, we will explore the role that physical activity and exercise play in achieving flow and unlocking your full potential.

09: Creating a Positive Mindset

Having a positive mindset is a critical component of achieving flow and living a fulfilling life. A positive mindset involves looking at the world and yourself in a positive light, and embracing a growth-oriented perspective that emphasizes personal development and growth. When you have a positive mindset, you are more resilient in the face of challenges and setbacks, and you are more likely to see opportunities and potential for growth in every situation.

Creating a positive mindset requires a conscious effort and a commitment to personal growth. The following are some tips for creating a positive mindset:

– Practice gratitude: Cultivate a sense of gratitude by focusing on the things that you are grateful for in your life. Write a daily gratitude journal, and reflect on the things that you are grateful for each day. This simple act of reflection can help you to cultivate a more positive mindset and a greater appreciation for all that you have in your life.

– Focus on the present: One of the keys to a positive mindset is to focus on the present moment. The present moment is where all of our power and potential lies, and focusing on the present moment can help us to release negative thoughts and emotions and embrace a more positive perspective.

– Surround yourself with positive people: The people that you surround yourself with have a huge impact on your thoughts and emotions. Surround yourself with people who are positive, supportive, and who share your values and goals. Avoid spending time with people who are negative or who bring you down.

– Embrace positivity: Choose to focus on the positive aspects of life, rather than the negative. When you find yourself focusing on negative thoughts or feelings, take a step back and reframe your perspective. Focus on the positive aspects of a situation, and look for opportunities for growth and improvement.

– Cultivate a growth mindset: Embrace a growth-oriented perspective, and focus on personal development and growth. Rather than focusing on your limitations and weaknesses, focus on your strengths and areas of potential. Believe in your ability to grow and improve, and embrace the challenges that come your way as opportunities for growth and learning.

09: CREATING A POSITIVE MINDSET

– Practice self-compassion: Be kind and compassionate with yourself, and avoid being overly critical or self-judgmental. Practice self-compassion by accepting yourself for who you are, and embracing your limitations and imperfections as part of your unique journey.

– Focus on the good: Make it a habit to focus on the good in every situation, no matter how small. By focusing on the good, you can cultivate a more positive outlook and a greater appreciation for life.

In conclusion, creating a positive mindset is a critical component of achieving flow and unlocking your full potential. By embracing a growth-oriented perspective, focusing on the present moment, surrounding yourself with positive people, and practicing gratitude, self-compassion, and positivity, you can cultivate a positive mindset and achieve flow in all areas of your life. In the next chapter, we will explore the role that mindfulness and meditation play in achieving flow and unlocking your full potential.

10: Using Visualization to Achieve Your Goals

Visualization is a powerful technique that involves using your imagination to create vivid, mental images of your goals and aspirations. By visualizing your desired outcomes, you can activate the power of your subconscious mind and increase your motivation and drive to achieve your goals.

Visualization is based on the principle that our thoughts and emotions have a direct impact on our behavior and our ability to achieve our goals. By visualizing your goals, you can tap into the power of your subconscious mind and create a clear and focused plan for achieving your desired outcomes.

The following are some tips for using visualization to achieve your goals:

– Get clear on your goals: Before you start visualizing, it is important to get clear on your goals. Take some time to reflect on what you really want to achieve in your life, and write down your goals in a clear and concise manner.

– Create vivid, mental images: When you visualize your

goals, it is important to create vivid, mental images of your desired outcomes. Use all of your senses to create a clear and detailed picture in your mind, and imagine what it would feel like to achieve your goals.

– Make it a daily practice: Make visualization a daily practice by setting aside some time each day to focus on your goals. You can visualize first thing in the morning, before you go to bed, or whenever you have some quiet time to yourself.

– Use positive affirmations: Along with visualization, use positive affirmations to reinforce your desired outcomes. Repeat positive affirmations to yourself, such as "I am successful," "I am confident," or "I am capable of achieving my goals."

– Believe in your abilities: To make visualization effective, you must believe in your abilities to achieve your goals. Embrace a growth-oriented perspective, and focus on your strengths and potential. Believe in your ability to overcome challenges and obstacles, and have faith in yourself.

– Stay focused: Keep your focus on your goals, and avoid letting negative thoughts or distractions get in the way.

10: USING VISUALIZATION TO ACHIEVE YOUR GOALS

Visualize your goals daily, and stay focused on your desired outcomes.

– Stay flexible: Be open to new possibilities, and remain flexible in your approach to achieving your goals. Be willing to adjust your goals as needed, and embrace new opportunities as they arise.

In conclusion, visualization is a powerful tool for achieving your goals and unlocking your full potential. By creating vivid, mental images of your desired outcomes, you can tap into the power of your subconscious mind and increase your motivation and drive to achieve your goals. Remember to get clear on your goals, make visualization a daily practice, use positive affirmations, believe in your abilities, stay focused, and stay flexible, and you will be on your way to achieving your goals and living a fulfilling life. In the next chapter, we will explore the role that exercise and physical activity play in achieving flow and unlocking your full potential.

11: Embracing the Power of Gratitude

Gratitude is a powerful tool for transforming your life and unlocking your full potential. When we cultivate an attitude of gratitude, we shift our focus away from what we don't have and towards what we do have. This shift in perspective can have a profound impact on our happiness, well-being, and success.

The following are some benefits of embracing the power of gratitude:

– Increased happiness: Studies have shown that people who practice gratitude regularly experience increased levels of happiness and well-being. When we focus on what we are thankful for, we are more likely to experience feelings of joy, peace, and contentment.

– Improved relationships: Gratitude can also improve our relationships by helping us to be more appreciative of others and to focus on the positive aspects of our interactions. By expressing gratitude towards others, we can strengthen our bonds and create more positive and fulfilling relationships.

11: EMBRACING THE POWER OF GRATITUDE

– Better health: Gratitude has also been linked to better health outcomes. People who practice gratitude regularly experience lower levels of stress, improved sleep, and a stronger immune system.

– Increased motivation and success: Gratitude can also increase our motivation and drive to succeed. When we focus on what we are thankful for, we are more likely to be motivated to work towards our goals, and we are more likely to experience success in our personal and professional lives.

The following are some tips for incorporating gratitude into your daily life:

– Keep a gratitude journal: One of the best ways to cultivate gratitude is to keep a gratitude journal. Each day, write down three things that you are grateful for. This could be anything from a beautiful sunset, to a supportive friend, to a warm meal.

– Practice mindfulness: Mindfulness can also help you to cultivate gratitude. Take time each day to focus on your breath, and pay attention to the present moment. When you are mindful, you are more likely to experience feelings of gratitude and appreciation.

11: EMBRACING THE POWER OF GRATITUDE

– Express gratitude to others: Another way to cultivate gratitude is to express gratitude to others. Write a thank you note to someone who has impacted your life, or tell a friend or family member how much you appreciate them.

– Focus on the positives: Make it a habit to focus on the positives in your life, rather than the negatives. When you focus on the good things in your life, you are more likely to experience feelings of gratitude and happiness.

– Give back: Finally, consider giving back to others. Whether it's volunteering your time, making a donation, or simply performing a random act of kindness, giving back can help you to cultivate gratitude and experience the joy of making a positive impact on others.

In conclusion, embracing the power of gratitude can have a profound impact on your happiness, well-being, and success. By focusing on what you are thankful for, expressing gratitude towards others, and incorporating gratitude into your daily life, you can unlock the full power of gratitude and transform your life for the better. In the next chapter, we will explore the role of creativity and play in achieving flow and unlocking your full potential.

12: Building Strong Relationships

Strong relationships play a crucial role in our lives. They provide us with love, support, and a sense of belonging. When we have strong, positive relationships, we are more likely to experience feelings of happiness, well-being, and success.

The following are some benefits of building strong relationships:

– Increased happiness: Studies have shown that people with strong relationships experience higher levels of happiness and well-being. When we have positive relationships, we are more likely to experience feelings of joy, contentment, and peace.

– Improved health: Strong relationships can also improve our physical health. People with positive relationships are less likely to experience stress, and they are more likely to experience better sleep, a stronger immune system, and a lower risk of chronic disease.

– Increased motivation and success: Strong relationships can also increase our motivation and drive to succeed. When we have supportive relationships, we are more likely to feel encouraged and motivated to work towards our goals, and we are more likely to experience success in our personal and professional lives.

The following are some tips for building strong relationships:

– Communication: One of the key components of strong relationships is effective communication. Take the time to listen to your loved ones, and express yourself in a clear and respectful manner. When we communicate effectively, we are more likely to build positive relationships.

– Shared interests: Another way to build strong relationships is to find shared interests. Whether it's a shared hobby, a love of a particular sport, or a shared passion for a particular cause, finding shared interests can help you to build stronger relationships.

– Quality time: Spending quality time with your loved ones is also crucial for building strong relationships. Whether it's a family dinner, a game night, or a weekend getaway, taking the time to spend with your loved ones can help you to build stronger relationships.

– Empathy and understanding: Empathy and understanding are also key components of strong relationships. When we are able to understand and empathize with others, we are more likely to build positive relationships.

– Give and take: Finally, building strong relationships requires give and take. Be willing to compromise and support others, and expect the same in return. When we are able to give and take, we are more likely to build strong, positive relationships.

In conclusion, building strong relationships is crucial for our happiness, well-being, and success. By taking the time to communicate effectively, finding shared interests, spending quality time with loved ones, showing empathy and understanding, and engaging in give and take, you can build strong, positive relationships that will support you in all areas of your life. In the next chapter, we will explore the role of exercise and physical activity in achieving flow and unlocking your full potential.

13: The Benefits of a Healthy Lifestyle

A healthy lifestyle is essential for achieving flow and unlocking our full potential. When we take care of our bodies and minds, we are better able to focus, think clearly, and experience positive emotions. In this chapter, we will explore the benefits of a healthy lifestyle, and how it can help us to achieve flow.

— Improved physical health: A healthy lifestyle can lead to improved physical health. Eating a balanced diet, getting regular exercise, and getting enough sleep can help to boost our energy levels, improve our immune system, and lower our risk of chronic diseases such as heart disease, diabetes, and certain types of cancer.

— Increased mental clarity: A healthy lifestyle can also improve our mental clarity. Eating a nutritious diet, getting regular exercise, and getting enough sleep can help to improve our concentration, focus, and memory.

— Improved mood: A healthy lifestyle can also improve our mood. Regular exercise, eating a nutritious diet, and getting enough sleep can help to boost our mood and reduce stress, anxiety, and depression.

– Increased confidence: A healthy lifestyle can also increase our confidence. When we feel good physically, we are more likely to feel good about ourselves, and to have the confidence to tackle new challenges and opportunities.

– Better sleep: A healthy lifestyle can also lead to better sleep. Eating a nutritious diet, getting regular exercise, and reducing stress can help us to sleep better, and to wake up feeling refreshed and energized.

The following are some tips for incorporating a healthy lifestyle into your life:

– Eating a balanced diet: Eating a balanced diet that includes plenty of fruits, vegetables, whole grains, and lean protein can help to provide your body with the nutrients it needs to function optimally.

– Regular exercise: Regular exercise, such as brisk walking, running, cycling, or swimming, can help to improve your physical health, boost your mood, and reduce stress.

– Getting enough sleep: Getting enough sleep is also essential for a healthy lifestyle. Aim for 7-9 hours of sleep per night, and create a bedtime routine that includes winding down and disconnecting from electronic devices.

– Managing stress: Managing stress is also crucial for a healthy lifestyle. Engage in stress-reducing activities such as mindfulness, yoga, or deep breathing, and make time for relaxation and self-care.

– Staying hydrated: Staying hydrated is also essential for a healthy lifestyle. Aim to drink at least 8 glasses of water per day, and avoid sugary drinks and caffeine.

In conclusion, a healthy lifestyle is crucial for achieving flow and unlocking our full potential. By eating a balanced diet, engaging in regular exercise, getting enough sleep, managing stress, and staying hydrated, you can improve your physical and mental health, boost your mood, and increase your confidence. In the next chapter, we will explore the role of nature and the environment in achieving flow.

14: Nourishing Your Body with the Right Foods

Eating a nutritious diet is an important part of achieving flow and unlocking your full potential. The food we eat has a direct impact on our physical and mental health, and can either help or hinder our ability to experience flow. In this chapter, we will explore the role of diet in achieving flow, and how to nourish your body with the right foods.

– The Importance of a Nutritious Diet: A nutritious diet is essential for optimal physical and mental health. It provides our bodies with the nutrients and energy it needs to function at its best, and can help to improve our mood, boost our energy levels, and reduce our risk of chronic diseases.

– Understanding Macronutrients: Macronutrients are the main components of our diets, including carbohydrates, protein, and fat. Understanding the role of these macronutrients and how they impact our bodies is important for maintaining a balanced and nutritious diet.

– The Benefits of Eating a Plant-Based Diet: A diet that is rich in whole, plant-based foods can provide your body with all the nutrients it needs to function optimally. Eating a variety of fruits, vegetables, whole grains, and legumes can help to reduce your risk of chronic diseases, improve your digestion, and boost your mood.

– The Risks of Processed Foods: Processed foods are often high in added sugars, salt, and unhealthy fats, and can be harmful to our health. Limiting processed foods in your diet and choosing whole, nutritious foods instead can help to improve your physical and mental health.

– Eating for Energy: Eating nutrient-dense, energy-boosting foods, such as complex carbohydrates, lean protein, and healthy fats, can help to improve your energy levels, and support your ability to experience flow.

The following are some tips for nourishing your body with the right foods:

– Eating a variety of whole, plant-based foods: Aim to eat a variety of fruits, vegetables, whole grains, and legumes, to provide your body with a wide range of essential nutrients.

– Limiting processed foods: Limiting processed foods in your diet, and choosing whole, nutritious foods instead, can help to improve your physical and mental health.

— Hydrating with water: Staying hydrated is essential for optimal physical and mental health. Aim to drink at least 8 glasses of water per day, and limit your intake of sugary drinks and caffeine.

— Planning ahead: Planning ahead, and preparing healthy meals and snacks in advance, can help to ensure that you are always nourishing your body with the right foods.

— Listening to your body: Paying attention to your body's signals, and eating when you are hungry, and stopping when you are full, can help you to eat mindfully, and to make healthier food choices.

In conclusion, nourishing your body with the right foods is essential for achieving flow and unlocking your full potential. Eating a balanced and nutritious diet, that is rich in whole, plant-based foods, and low in processed foods, can improve your physical and mental health, boost your energy levels, and support your ability to experience flow. In the next chapter, we will explore the role of exercise in achieving flow.

15: The Role of Exercise in Achieving Flow

Exercise is an essential part of achieving flow and unlocking your full potential. Physical activity can help to improve your physical and mental health, and can be a powerful tool for achieving a state of flow. In this chapter, we will explore the role of exercise in achieving flow, and how to incorporate physical activity into your daily routine.

– The Physical Benefits of Exercise: Regular exercise can help to improve your physical health by reducing your risk of chronic diseases, such as heart disease and diabetes, and improving your cardiovascular health. Exercise can also help to improve your strength, flexibility, and endurance.

– The Mental Benefits of Exercise: Exercise has been shown to have a positive impact on our mental health, and can help to reduce stress, anxiety, and depression. Exercise can also help to improve our mood, and boost our cognitive function.

– The Benefits of High-Intensity Interval Training (HIIT): High-intensity interval training (HIIT) is a form of exercise that alternates between periods of high-intensity exercise and periods of rest. HIIT has been shown to be particularly effective for improving cardiovascular health and boosting weight loss.

– The Benefits of Mind-Body Exercises: Mind-body exercises, such as yoga and tai chi, can help to improve our physical and mental health, and can be particularly effective for reducing stress and anxiety.

– The Benefits of Outdoor Exercise: Outdoor exercise can provide numerous physical and mental health benefits, and can help to improve our connection with nature and our environment.

The following are some tips for incorporating exercise into your daily routine:

– Finding an activity you enjoy: Finding an exercise activity that you enjoy, such as dancing, swimming, or hiking, can make it easier to stick to a regular exercise routine.

– Making exercise a priority: Incorporating exercise into your daily routine, and making it a priority, can help to ensure that you are getting the physical and mental health benefits of exercise.

15: THE ROLE OF EXERCISE IN ACHIEVING FLOW

– Incorporating variety: Mixing up your exercise routine, and incorporating a variety of activities, can help to prevent boredom, and to improve your physical and mental health.

– Setting realistic goals: Setting realistic exercise goals, such as aiming to exercise for 30 minutes a day, or to complete a specific workout, can help to keep you motivated.

– Exercising with a friend or group: Exercising with a friend or group can provide social support, and can make exercise more enjoyable.

In conclusion, exercise is an essential part of achieving flow and unlocking your full potential. Regular exercise can help to improve your physical and mental health, and can be a powerful tool for achieving a state of flow. In the next chapter, we will explore the role of sleep in achieving flow.

16: The Benefits of Meditation

Meditation is a powerful tool for achieving flow and unlocking your full potential. Meditation is a practice that involves focusing your mind on a particular object, thought, or activity, to improve awareness and achieve mental clarity. In this chapter, we will explore the benefits of meditation, and how to incorporate meditation into your daily routine.

— The Physical Benefits of Meditation: Meditation has been shown to have numerous physical health benefits, including reducing stress, improving cardiovascular health, and boosting the immune system. Meditation has also been shown to help with sleep problems, chronic pain, and anxiety.

— The Mental Benefits of Meditation: Meditation has been shown to have a positive impact on our mental health, and can help to reduce stress, anxiety, and depression. Meditation can also help to improve our mood, and boost our cognitive function.

— The Spiritual Benefits of Meditation: Meditation can help to connect you with your inner self and provide a sense of inner peace and calm. It can also help to improve your spiritual awareness, and provide a deeper understanding of your place in the world.

– The Benefits of Mindfulness Meditation: Mindfulness meditation is a type of meditation that involves focusing on the present moment, and accepting and observing your thoughts and feelings without judgment. Mindfulness meditation has been shown to be particularly effective for reducing stress and improving mental health.

– The Benefits of Transcendental Meditation: Transcendental meditation is a type of meditation that involves repeating a mantra, or word, to help achieve a deep state of relaxation and mental clarity. Transcendental meditation has been shown to be effective for reducing stress and improving mental health.

The following are some tips for incorporating meditation into your daily routine:

– Finding a quiet place: Finding a quiet place to meditate, free from distractions, can help to improve the quality of your meditation practice.

– Making meditation a priority: Incorporating meditation into your daily routine, and making it a priority, can help to ensure that you are getting the physical and mental health benefits of meditation.

– Starting with short sessions: Starting with short meditation sessions, such as 5-10 minutes, and gradually increasing the length of your meditation sessions can help to prevent boredom and ensure that you are getting the full benefits of meditation.

– Incorporating guided meditations: Incorporating guided meditations, such as those found on meditation apps or YouTube, can help to provide structure and guidance to your meditation practice.

– Setting realistic goals: Setting realistic meditation goals, such as aiming to meditate for 10 minutes a day, can help to keep you motivated.

In conclusion, meditation is a powerful tool for achieving flow and unlocking your full potential. Meditation has been shown to have numerous physical and mental health benefits, and can help to provide a sense of inner peace and calm. In the next chapter, we will explore the role of positive affirmations in achieving flow.

17: The Power of Affirmations

Affirmations are powerful statements that can help to change the way we think and feel about ourselves and our lives. Affirmations are positive statements that can help to reprogram our subconscious mind and improve our mental and emotional state. In this chapter, we will explore the power of affirmations and how to use affirmations to achieve flow.

– What are Affirmations: Affirmations are positive statements that can help to change the way we think and feel about ourselves and our lives. Affirmations can help to reprogram our subconscious mind and improve our mental and emotional state.

– The Science Behind Affirmations: Affirmations work by changing the neural pathways in our brain, and shifting our focus to a more positive and empowering perspective. This shift in perspective can help to improve our mood, increase our self-confidence, and boost our overall well-being.

– The Benefits of Using Affirmations: Using affirmations can help to improve our mental and emotional state, and increase our self-confidence and self-esteem. Affirmations can also help to improve our physical health, as our thoughts and emotions are closely tied to our physical state.

— How to Use Affirmations: There are several ways to use affirmations, including repeating affirmations to yourself several times a day, writing affirmations down, and visualizing affirmations. You can also use affirmations in combination with other tools, such as visualization and meditation, to increase their effectiveness.

— Examples of Affirmations: There are many different types of affirmations that you can use, and the best affirmations for you will depend on your individual needs and goals. Some examples of affirmations include "I am capable and worthy of achieving my goals," "I am strong and resilient," and "I am surrounded by love and positivity."

The following are some tips for incorporating affirmations into your daily routine:

— Make affirmations a daily habit: Incorporating affirmations into your daily routine, and making it a daily habit, can help to ensure that you are getting the full benefits of affirmations.

— Repeat affirmations several times a day: Repeating affirmations several times a day, and throughout the day, can help to reinforce the positive statements and improve their effectiveness.

– Write affirmations down: Writing affirmations down, and keeping them in a place where you can see them often, can help to reinforce the positive statements and improve their effectiveness.

– Visualize affirmations: Visualizing affirmations, and imagining yourself in the situation that the affirmation is describing, can help to increase their effectiveness and make them feel more real.

– Choose affirmations that resonate with you: Choosing affirmations that resonate with you, and that align with your individual goals and values, can help to increase their effectiveness and make them feel more meaningful.

In conclusion, affirmations are powerful tools that can help to change the way we think and feel about ourselves and our lives. Affirmations can help to improve our mental and emotional state, and increase our self-confidence and self-esteem. In the next chapter, we will explore the role of goal-setting in achieving flow.

18: The Art of Forgiveness

Forgiveness is a powerful tool that can have a transformative effect on our lives. It is a way of letting go of negative feelings and resentment towards someone who has wronged us, allowing us to move forward with a positive and open mind.

Forgiveness is not just about letting the other person off the hook. It is about releasing ourselves from the grip of negative emotions and finding peace within ourselves. Holding onto anger and resentment can be toxic to our mental and physical health, causing feelings of stress and anxiety, and even leading to physical symptoms like high blood pressure and heart disease.

Forgiving someone does not mean forgetting what has happened, or condoning their actions. It is simply a way of letting go of the emotional baggage that can hold us back. When we forgive, we free ourselves from the negative emotions that can prevent us from living in the moment and experiencing flow.

The process of forgiveness is often a personal journey, and can take time and effort. But it can be a life-changing experience, allowing us to find inner peace and happiness, and move forward with a positive and optimistic outlook.

There are several strategies that can help us on the path to forgiveness, including writing letters to the person we need to forgive, practicing mindfulness and self-reflection, and seeking the help of a counselor or therapist.

Forgiveness is an essential part of living in the moment and unlocking our full potential with the principles of flow. It is a way of freeing ourselves from the negative emotions that can hold us back, and allowing us to focus on the present moment and find joy and fulfillment in life.

19: Finding Your Passion and Purpose

Life is a journey, and it's up to each of us to determine what that journey will look like. Whether you're just starting out or are well into adulthood, the search for your passion and purpose is one that is both exciting and challenging. But what exactly is passion and purpose, and how can you find them?

Passion refers to a strong feeling of excitement and enthusiasm for something, often a particular activity or interest. It's something that you're naturally drawn to and that provides a sense of fulfillment and satisfaction. Purpose, on the other hand, is a sense of meaning and direction in your life. It's a reason for why you do what you do, a driving force that gives you a sense of purpose and direction.

The two are often intertwined and can be found together, but they don't always have to be. You may have a passion for something that doesn't necessarily align with your purpose, or vice versa. Finding both, however, can bring a sense of balance and fulfillment to your life.

So, how do you find your passion and purpose? Here are a

few tips to get started:

Get to know yourself: Take some time to reflect on who you are and what makes you unique. What are your strengths and weaknesses, your likes and dislikes, and what do you value most in life? This self-reflection can help you identify your passions and what you're naturally drawn to.

Experiment: Don't be afraid to try new things. Whether it's taking a class, trying a new hobby, or volunteering, exposing yourself to new experiences can help you discover what you're truly passionate about.

Follow your intuition: Trust your gut and listen to your inner voice. If something feels right, it probably is. If you're feeling drawn to a particular activity or interest, don't ignore it. Pursue it and see where it takes you.

Surround yourself with positivity: Surrounding yourself with positive and supportive people can help you stay motivated and encouraged as you search for your passion and purpose. Seek out individuals who are uplifting and encouraging, and who will support you on your journey.

Embrace the power of flow: Flow is the state of being completely absorbed in an activity, where time seems to stand still and you are fully present in the moment. When you're in flow, you're completely focused on what you're doing and it brings a sense of joy and fulfillment. Finding activities that allow you to enter this state can help you identify your passions and purpose.

By following these tips and embracing the power of flow, you'll be well on your way to finding your passion and purpose. Remember, the journey is just as important as the destination, so don't be discouraged if it takes some time. Just keep moving forward and trust that you'll find what you're looking for.

In conclusion, finding your passion and purpose is a journey that requires self-reflection, experimentation, and a willingness to embrace the power of positive energy. With these tools in hand, you'll be able to transform your life and unlock your full potential. So, start your journey today and discover what truly brings you joy, fulfillment, and a sense of meaning in your life.

20: The Importance of Setting Goals

One of the key components of living a fulfilling and purposeful life is setting goals. Goals provide direction and a roadmap for where you want to go, and they help you measure your progress along the way. But goal-setting is more than just a way to track your progress, it is an essential part of unlocking your full potential and living life to the fullest. In this chapter, we'll explore the importance of setting goals and how the principles of flow can help you achieve success.

Why Set Goals?

Goals serve several important functions in our lives. First, they provide a sense of direction and purpose. When you have a clear destination in mind, you're more likely to stay focused and motivated. Goals also give you a way to measure your progress, so you can see the results of your hard work and adjust your strategy as needed.

Another important aspect of goal-setting is that it helps you prioritize your time and resources. When you have a clear set of goals, you can allocate your time and energy more effectively, ensuring that you're making the most of each day.

Goals also help you stay organized and focused, which can reduce stress and increase productivity.

Finally, goal-setting can be a powerful motivator. When you set achievable goals for yourself, you're more likely to stay motivated and push yourself to achieve more. The sense of accomplishment that comes from reaching your goals can be incredibly empowering and can lead to greater self-confidence and a sense of personal growth.

The Power of Flow in Goal-Setting

The principles of flow can play a significant role in helping you achieve your goals. Flow is the state of being completely absorbed in an activity, where time seems to stand still and you're fully present in the moment. When you're in flow, you're more likely to be productive, focused, and motivated.

Here are a few ways that flow can help you achieve your goals:

– Increased focus: Flow helps you stay focused and present in the moment, which is essential for achieving your goals. When you're in flow, you're less likely to be distracted by external factors and can instead concentrate fully on what you're doing.

– Improved motivation: Flow brings a sense of joy and ful-fillment that can help you stay motivated and driven, even when the going gets tough. When you're in flow, you're more likely to push yourself to achieve more, and the sense of accomplishment that comes from reaching your goals can be incredibly empowering.

– Better time management: Flow helps you manage your time more effectively, so you can allocate your resources and prioritize your goals. When you're in flow, you're more likely to be productive and focused, and less likely to waste time on unimportant tasks.

– Increased creativity: Flow can help you tap into your cre-ativity and come up with new and innovative ideas. When you're in flow, your mind is free to explore new possibilities and find creative solutions to the challenges you face.

– Reduced stress: Flow has been shown to reduce stress and increase overall well-being. When you're in flow, you're more likely to feel relaxed and focused, which can help you stay motivated and reduce stress levels.

In conclusion, goal-setting is an essential part of living a fulfilling and purposeful life. By setting achievable goals and embracing the principles of flow, you can unlock your full potential and achieve success in all areas of your life. So, take the time to set your goals and start your journey today, and discover what it means to truly live life to the fullest.

21: Creating a Vision Board

One of the most powerful tools for achieving your goals and unlocking your full potential is creating a vision board. A vision board is a visual representation of your goals and aspirations, and it can help you focus your mind, stay motivated, and bring your dreams to life. In this chapter, we'll explore the power of vision boards and how the principles of flow can help you create and use this powerful tool to achieve success.

What is a Vision Board?

A vision board is a collage of images, words, and other visual elements that represent your goals, aspirations, and dreams. You can create a vision board on a physical board or as a digital collage, and it can be as simple or complex as you like. The goal of a vision board is to help you focus your mind and stay motivated, so you can bring your dreams to life.

Why Create a Vision Board?

There are many reasons why creating a vision board can be an effective tool for achieving your goals. First, vision boards help you focus your mind and stay motivated. When you have a visual representation of your goals and aspirations, it's easier to stay focused and motivated, even when the going gets tough.

Second, vision boards help you tap into the power of positive energy and the principles of flow. When you create a vision board, you're visualizing your future and aligning your mind with your goals. This can help you tap into the power of positive energy and attract the right opportunities, resources, and people into your life.

Third, vision boards can help you overcome obstacles and stay on track. When you have a visual representation of your goals, it's easier to stay focused and motivated, even when faced with challenges.

Finally, vision boards can help you create a sense of accountability. When you have a visual representation of your goals, it's easier to stay focused and motivated, and you're more likely to hold yourself accountable for achieving your goals.

How to Create a Vision Board

Creating a vision board is a fun and simple process, and it's a great way to tap into the power of positive energy and the principles of flow. Here are the steps for creating your vision board:

– your materials: To create your vision board, you'll need a physical board or a digital platform, a collection of images and words that represent your goals and aspirations, and a few basic supplies like glue, scissors, and markers.

– Identify your goals: Before you start creating your vision board, it's important to identify your goals and aspirations. Take some time to reflect on what you really want to achieve, and make a list of your goals and aspirations.

– Gather images and words: Once you've identified your goals, start gathering images and words that represent your aspirations. Look for images and words that inspire you and resonate with your goals. You can find inspiration from magazines, books, the internet, or anywhere else that you find inspiring.

– Create your board: Once you have your images and words, it's time to create your vision board. You can create a physical board by glueing your images and words onto a piece of poster board or canvas, or you can create a digital vision board using a platform like Canva or PicMonkey.

– Review and refine: Once you've created your vision board, take a few moments to review and refine it. Make sure that it represents your goals and aspirations, and that it inspires and motivates you.

Using Your Vision Board to Achieve Your Goals

Once you've created your vision board, it's important to use it to achieve your goals. Here are a few tips for using your vision board to tap into the power of positive energy and the principles of flow:

– Place your vision board in a prominent location: To get the most out of your vision board, place it in a location where you can see it every day. This will help you stay focused and motivated, and it will help you tap into the power of positive energy.

– Review your vision board regularly: Regularly review your vision board and focus on the images and words that represent your goals and aspirations. This will help you stay focused and motivated, and it will help you tap into the power of positive energy.

21: CREATING A VISION BOARD

– Align your actions with your vision board: To achieve your goals, it's important to align your actions with your vision board. Take daily actions that move you closer to your goals, and use your vision board as a guide.

– Celebrate your progress: As you achieve your goals, take time to celebrate your progress. This will help you stay motivated and it will help you tap into the power of positive energy.

Conclusion

Creating a vision board is a powerful tool for achieving your goals and unlocking your full potential. By using the power of positive energy and the principles of flow, you can create a vision board that inspires and motivates you, and that helps you bring your dreams to life. So go ahead and start creating your vision board today, and tap into the power of positive energy to achieve success!

22: Overcoming Procrastination

Procrastination is one of the biggest obstacles to achieving success and unlocking our full potential. It can prevent us from reaching our goals, and it can sap our energy and motivation. But the good news is that procrastination can be overcome with the right mindset and approach. In this chapter, we'll explore the power of positive energy and the principles of flow, and how they can be used to overcome procrastination and unleash your full potential.

Understanding the Causes of Procrastination

Procrastination is often caused by a variety of factors, including fear of failure, lack of motivation, and a general sense of overwhelm. But at its core, procrastination is a self-sabotaging behavior that stems from a lack of focus and direction. When we procrastinate, we are effectively choosing to prioritize other things over the important tasks that will help us reach our goals.

The Power of Positive Energy

Positive energy is a powerful force that can help us overcome procrastination and unleash our full potential. Positive energy is the energy of positivity, motivation, and inspiration, and it can help us overcome the obstacles that hold us back. By focusing on positive energy, we can tap into our inner reserves of strength, motivation, and inspiration, and use them to achieve our goals.

The Principles of Flow

Flow is the state of being completely absorbed in a task or activity, and it's a key ingredient in overcoming procrastination and unlocking our full potential. When we are in flow, we are completely focused on the task at hand, and we are free from distractions and interruptions. This allows us to give our best effort and achieve great results.

Tips for Overcoming Procrastination with Positive Energy and Flow

— Set clear and specific goals: To overcome procrastination, it's important to set clear and specific goals. By setting specific, measurable, attainable, relevant, and time-bound (SMART) goals, you'll have a clear direction and focus, and you'll be more likely to overcome procrastination.

— Break down your goals into manageable tasks: Breaking down your goals into smaller, manageable tasks can help you overcome procrastination. When you have a clear and manageable plan, you'll be more likely to start working on your goals and avoid procrastination.

– Focus on positive energy: To overcome procrastination, it's important to focus on positive energy. Surround yourself with positive people, and focus on your strengths and positive qualities. By focusing on positive energy, you'll be more likely to overcome procrastination and reach your goals.

– Get into the flow: Flow is a powerful tool for overcoming procrastination. To get into flow, it's important to eliminate distractions and focus completely on the task at hand. When you're in flow, you'll be more likely to overcome procrastination and achieve great results.

Conclusion

Procrastination can be a major obstacle to achieving success and unlocking our full potential. But with the right mindset and approach, it can be overcome. By focusing on positive energy and the principles of flow, you can overcome procrastination and unleash your full potential. So start putting these tips into action today, and overcome procrastination to achieve your goals and live the life of your dreams!

23: Developing Resilience

Resilience is a critical quality that can help us overcome adversity and achieve our goals. It's the ability to bounce back from setbacks and challenges, and to maintain a positive outlook and approach even in the face of difficulty. In this chapter, we'll explore the power of positive energy and the principles of flow, and how they can be used to develop resilience and unlock your full potential.

The Importance of Resilience

Resilience is an essential quality for success, as it allows us to overcome adversity and maintain a positive outlook and approach even in the face of difficulty. With resilience, we can keep our spirits up and maintain our focus on our goals, even when things aren't going according to plan.

The Power of Positive Energy

Positive energy is a powerful force that can help us develop resilience and overcome adversity. Positive energy is the energy of positivity, motivation, and inspiration, and it can help us overcome the obstacles that hold us back. By focusing on positive energy, we can tap into our inner reserves of strength, motivation, and inspiration, and use them to achieve our goals.

The Principles of Flow

Flow is the state of being completely absorbed in a task or activity, and it's a key ingredient in developing resilience and unlocking our full potential. When we are in flow, we are completely focused on the task at hand, and we are free from distractions and interruptions. This allows us to give our best effort and achieve great results.

Tips for Developing Resilience with Positive Energy and Flow

– Focus on the present moment: To develop resilience, it's important to focus on the present moment. When we're focused on the present moment, we can maintain a positive outlook and approach, even in the face of adversity.

– Embrace change and uncertainty: Change and uncertainty are inevitable, but with resilience, we can embrace these challenges and turn them into opportunities for growth.

– Practice gratitude: Gratitude is a powerful tool for developing resilience. By focusing on the things we're thankful for, we can maintain a positive outlook and approach, even in the face of adversity.

– Get into the flow: Flow is a powerful tool for developing resilience. To get into flow, it's important to eliminate distractions and focus completely on the task at hand. When you're in flow, you'll be more likely to overcome adversity and achieve great results.

– Surround yourself with positive people: Surrounding yourself with positive people can help you maintain a positive outlook and approach, even in the face of adversity. Positive people can provide support and encouragement, and they can help you develop resilience.

Conclusion

Resilience is a critical quality that can help us overcome adversity and achieve our goals. By focusing on positive energy and the principles of flow, we can develop resilience and unleash our full potential. So start putting these tips into action today, and develop resilience to overcome adversity and achieve your goals!

24: Embracing Change

Introduction

Change is a constant in life. Whether it's a new job, a new relationship, or a new living situation, change is always happening around us. While change can be scary and overwhelming, it's also an opportunity for growth and transformation. In this chapter, we'll explore the power of positive energy and the principles of flow, and how they can be used to embrace change and unlock your full potential.

The Importance of Embracing Change

Change is inevitable and it's a part of life. Embracing change is critical because it allows us to grow and transform, both personally and professionally. By embracing change, we can break free from our comfort zones and explore new opportunities, which can lead to personal and professional growth.

The Power of Positive Energy

Positive energy is a powerful force that can help us embrace change and grow. Positive energy is the energy of positivity, motivation, and inspiration, and it can help us overcome the obstacles that hold us back. By focusing on positive energy, we can tap into our inner reserves of strength, motivation, and inspiration, and use them to achieve our goals.

The Principles of Flow

Flow is the state of being completely absorbed in a task or activity, and it's a key ingredient in embracing change and unlocking our full potential. When we are in flow, we are completely focused on the task at hand, and we are free from distractions and interruptions. This allows us to give our best effort and achieve great results, even in the face of change.

Tips for Embracing Change with Positive Energy and Flow

– Embrace change as an opportunity: To embrace change, it's important to view it as an opportunity for growth and transformation, rather than a threat.

– Focus on the present moment: To embrace change, it's important to focus on the present moment. When we're focused on the present moment, we can maintain a positive outlook and approach, even in the face of change.

– Practice gratitude: Gratitude is a powerful tool for embracing change. By focusing on the things we're thankful for, we can maintain a positive outlook and approach, even in the face of change.

– Get into the flow: Flow is a powerful tool for embracing change. To get into flow, it's important to eliminate distractions and focus completely on the task at hand. When you're in flow, you'll be more likely to embrace change and achieve great results.

– Surround yourself with positive people: Surrounding yourself with positive people can help you maintain a positive outlook and approach, even in the face of change. Positive people can provide support and encouragement, and they can help you embrace change.

Conclusion

Change is a constant in life, but it's also an opportunity for growth and transformation. By focusing on positive energy and the principles of flow, we can embrace change and unlock our full potential. So start putting these tips into action today, and embrace change to achieve your goals!

25: The Benefits of Travel and Adventure

Introduction

Travel and adventure can be a source of immense joy and growth. They offer the opportunity to step outside of our comfort zones, explore new cultures, and experience the world in new and exciting ways. In this chapter, we'll explore the benefits of travel and adventure, and how they can help us transform our lives with the power of positive energy and the principles of flow.

The Power of Positive Energy

Positive energy is a powerful force that can help us transform our lives and achieve our goals. Positive energy is the energy of positivity, motivation, and inspiration, and it can help us overcome the obstacles that hold us back. By focusing on positive energy, we can tap into our inner reserves of strength, motivation, and inspiration, and use them to achieve our goals.

The Principles of Flow

Flow is the state of being completely absorbed in a task or

activity, and it's a key ingredient in unlocking our full potential. When we are in flow, we are completely focused on the task at hand, and we are free from distractions and interruptions. This allows us to give our best effort and achieve great results, even in the face of new and challenging experiences.

The Benefits of Travel and Adventure

— New experiences and perspectives: Travel and adventure offer the opportunity to experience new cultures and perspectives, which can broaden our understanding of the world and help us grow as individuals.

— Personal growth: Travel and adventure can challenge us to step outside of our comfort zones and try new things, which can lead to personal growth and transformation.

— Building memories: Travel and adventure are a great way to build memories and create lasting experiences. Whether it's a scenic hike, a visit to a new city, or a trip to an exotic location, travel and adventure create memories that can last a lifetime.

— Increased confidence: Travel and adventure can help us

develop confidence, as we navigate new situations and overcome challenges. This can help us become more confident in our daily lives, and better equipped to handle new and challenging experiences.

– Increased creativity: Travel and adventure offer the opportunity to experience new and exciting things, which can stimulate our creativity and inspire new ideas.

Tips for Traveling and Adventuring with Positive Energy and Flow

– Embrace the unknown: To get the most out of travel and adventure, it's important to embrace the unknown. This means stepping outside of our comfort zones and embracing new and exciting experiences, even if they're a bit intimidating.

– Focus on the present moment: To get the most out of travel and adventure, it's important to focus on the present moment. When we're focused on the present moment, we can fully immerse ourselves in new experiences and create lasting memories.

– Practice gratitude: Gratitude is a powerful tool for enhancing the travel and adventure experience. By focusing on the things we're thankful for, we can maintain a positive outlook and approach, even in the face of new and challenging experiences.

– Get into the flow: Flow is a powerful tool for maximizing the travel and adventure experience. To get into flow, it's important to eliminate distractions and focus completely on the task at hand. Whether it's exploring a new city, hiking a scenic trail, or trying a new activity, flow can help us get the most out of our travel and adventure experiences.

– Plan ahead: Planning ahead can help ensure that your travel and adventure experiences are as enjoyable and successful as possible. Whether it's researching the best restaurants, mapping out your itinerary, or packing the right gear, planning ahead can help you make the most of your experiences.

Conclusion

Travel and adventure offer a unique opportunity to transform our lives with the power of positive energy and the principles of flow. By embracing new experiences, focusing on the present moment, practicing gratitude, getting into flow, and planning ahead, we can make the most of our travel and adventure experiences and achieve new levels of growth and transformation.

So if you're ready to take your life to the next level and transform it with the power of positive energy and the principles of flow, consider incorporating travel and adventure into your journey. Whether it's a trip to a new city, a scenic hike, or an exotic adventure, travel and adventure offer the opportunity to experience new and exciting things, broaden your perspective, and grow as an individual. So why not start planning your next adventure today and see where it takes you!

26: Finding Balance in Life

Finding balance in life can be a difficult task, but it's essential for living a happy and fulfilling life. In today's fast-paced world, it's easy to get caught up in our careers, relationships, and responsibilities and lose sight of what's truly important. However, by adopting the principles of flow and positive energy, we can achieve a sense of balance and harmony in all aspects of our lives.

One of the key components of finding balance in life is learning to prioritize our time and energy. This means taking a step back and evaluating what is truly important to us and making sure that we allocate our time and energy accordingly. This could mean spending more time with family and friends, dedicating more time to our hobbies and interests, or prioritizing self-care and personal development.

Another important aspect of finding balance in life is learning to manage stress and practice self-care. This could mean incorporating activities such as meditation, yoga, or journaling into your daily routine, or finding ways to incorporate more physical activity into your life. Additionally, taking time for yourself and engaging in activities that bring you joy and happiness can help to reduce stress and improve your overall well-being.

It's also important to remember that balance is not a static state, but a dynamic process that requires ongoing effort and attention. This means being open to making changes and adjusting our priorities as our lives evolve. For example, as our careers or personal circumstances change, we may need to readjust our priorities and allocate our time and energy differently.

In conclusion, finding balance in life is an essential component of living a happy and fulfilling life. By adopting the principles of flow and positive energy, we can prioritize our time and energy, manage stress, and engage in activities that bring us joy and happiness. Remember, balance is a dynamic process and requires ongoing effort, so don't be afraid to make changes and adjust your priorities as your life evolves.

27: Dealing with Stress

Stress is a natural part of life and can arise from a variety of sources, such as work, relationships, financial difficulties, and personal challenges. However, when stress becomes chronic, it can have a negative impact on our physical, mental, and emotional well-being. The good news is that by adopting the principles of flow and positive energy, we can learn to manage stress and maintain our well-being, even in challenging situations.

One of the most effective ways to manage stress is through mindfulness and meditation. Practicing mindfulness means paying attention to the present moment without judgment, and meditation involves focusing on the present moment and quieting the mind. By incorporating these practices into your daily routine, you can reduce stress and anxiety, improve your mental clarity, and increase your overall well-being.

Another effective way to manage stress is through physical activity. Exercise has been shown to reduce stress levels and improve mood by increasing the release of endorphins and other feel-good chemicals in the brain. Whether it's going for a walk, practicing yoga, or hitting the gym, incorporating physical activity into your daily routine can help you manage stress and maintain your overall well-being.

In addition to mindfulness and physical activity, it's important to maintain a healthy lifestyle. This means eating a balanced diet, getting enough sleep, and reducing alcohol and caffeine consumption. These habits can help you maintain your energy levels, reduce stress, and improve your overall well-being.

It's also important to learn coping mechanisms for dealing with stress in a healthy way. This could mean finding healthy outlets for your emotions, such as talking to a friend or therapist, practicing mindfulness, or engaging in activities that bring you joy and happiness. By developing healthy coping mechanisms, you can reduce stress and maintain your well-being even in challenging situations.

Finally, it's important to remember that stress is a natural part of life, and that it's okay to experience stress from time to time. By embracing the principles of flow and positive energy, we can learn to manage stress in a healthy way and maintain our well-being, even in challenging situations.

In conclusion, stress is a natural part of life, but when it becomes chronic it can have a negative impact on our well-be-ing. By adopting the principles of flow and positive energy, we can learn to manage stress through mindfulness, phys-ical activity, healthy lifestyle habits, and healthy coping mechanisms. Remember, it's okay to experience stress from time to time, and by embracing the principles of flow and positive energy, we can maintain our well-being and over-come stress in a healthy way.

28: Building Confidence

Confidence is an essential aspect of our lives, affecting our relationships, careers, and overall happiness. Without confidence, we may struggle to pursue our dreams and reach our full potential. Fortunately, by embracing the principles of flow and positive energy, we can build confidence and achieve our goals.

One of the most effective ways to build confidence is through self-reflection. By taking time to reflect on our strengths and weaknesses, we can gain a better understanding of who we are and what we want to achieve. This self-awareness can help us build confidence by providing us with a sense of direction and purpose.

Another important aspect of building confidence is taking care of our physical well-being. This means getting enough sleep, eating a healthy diet, and engaging in physical activity. When we feel good physically, we're more likely to feel confident and capable of achieving our goals.

It's also important to set and achieve achievable goals. This means starting small and gradually working towards larger goals. By successfully achieving our goals, we build confidence and become more capable of pursuing our dreams.

28: BUILDING CONFIDENCE

In addition to self-reflection and taking care of our physical well-being, it's important to surround ourselves with positive and supportive people. Having supportive friends and family can provide us with encouragement and help us build confidence in our abilities.

Finally, it's important to practice self-compassion. This means being kind and understanding with ourselves, even when we make mistakes. By embracing self-compassion, we can build confidence and avoid the negative effects of self-criticism and perfectionism.

In conclusion, confidence is an essential aspect of our lives, affecting our relationships, careers, and overall happiness. By embracing the principles of flow and positive energy, we can build confidence through self-reflection, taking care of our physical well-being, setting and achieving achievable goals, surrounding ourselves with positive and supportive people, and practicing self-compassion. Remember, building confidence takes time and effort, but by embracing the principles of flow and positive energy, we can achieve our goals and reach our full potential.

29: The Benefits of Volunteering and Giving Back

Volunteering and giving back to others are powerful ways to transform our lives and unleash our full potential. By embracing the principles of flow and positive energy, we can experience the many benefits that come from helping others and making a difference in the world.

One of the most significant benefits of volunteering and giving back is the increased sense of purpose and fulfillment that it brings. When we help others, we experience a sense of satisfaction and meaning that is often lacking in our daily lives. This sense of purpose can help us find a deeper sense of meaning and significance, which can lead to increased happiness and well-being.

Another benefit of volunteering and giving back is the opportunity to develop new skills and gain new experiences. By volunteering in areas that interest us or that challenge us, we can learn new skills, develop new perspectives, and gain a greater appreciation for the world around us. This can help us grow and develop as individuals, leading to increased personal and professional success.

29: THE BENEFITS OF VOLUNTEERING AND GIVING BACK

In addition, volunteering and giving back can help us build stronger relationships and connections with others. By working with others to achieve a common goal, we can build new relationships and strengthen existing ones. This can lead to increased social support and a greater sense of community, which is important for our overall health and well-being.

Finally, volunteering and giving back can have a positive impact on our mental health. Studies have shown that volunteering and helping others can reduce stress, improve mood, and increase feelings of happiness and well-being. This is because helping others releases endorphins and other feel-good chemicals in our brain, which can improve our overall sense of happiness and well-being.

In conclusion, volunteering and giving back are powerful ways to transform our lives and unleash our full potential. By embracing the principles of flow and positive energy, we can experience the many benefits that come from helping others, including increased purpose and fulfillment, new skills and experiences, stronger relationships and connections, and improved mental health. Remember, by volunteering and giving back, we can make a positive impact in the world and live our lives to the fullest.

30: The Power of Positive Thinking

Positive thinking is a powerful tool that can help us transform our lives and unlock our full potential. By embracing the principles of flow and positive energy, we can harness the power of positive thinking to improve our happiness, well-being, and overall success.

Positive thinking is the act of focusing on the positive aspects of our lives and viewing challenges and setbacks as opportunities for growth and learning. By doing so, we can overcome obstacles and achieve our goals more effectively. Positive thinking also allows us to approach life with a sense of hope and optimism, which can help us deal with stress and adversity more effectively.

One of the key benefits of positive thinking is increased happiness and well-being. Positive thinking helps us to focus on the good in our lives, rather than dwelling on the negative. This can improve our overall mood and increase feelings of happiness and contentment. Positive thinking also helps us to develop a more positive outlook on life, which can lead to increased resilience and the ability to bounce back from adversity more effectively.

Another benefit of positive thinking is improved relation-ships. Positive thinking can help us to communicate more effectively and build stronger relationships with others. By approaching interactions with a positive attitude, we can create a more supportive and empowering environment for ourselves and those around us. This can lead to greater suc-cess in both personal and professional relationships.

In addition, positive thinking can have a positive impact on our mental and physical health. Research has shown that positive thinking can help to reduce stress, improve im-mune function, and increase feelings of happiness and well-being. This is because positive thinking helps to release en-dorphins and other feel-good chemicals in our brain, which can improve our overall sense of happiness and well-being.

Finally, positive thinking can help us to achieve our goals more effectively. By focusing on the positive and viewing challenges as opportunities for growth and learning, we can approach our goals with a sense of confidence and determ-ination. This can help us to overcome obstacles and achieve success more quickly and effectively.

In conclusion, positive thinking is a powerful tool that can help us transform our lives and unlock our full potential. By embracing the principles of flow and positive energy, we can harness the power of positive thinking to improve our happiness, well-being, relationships, health, and overall success. Remember, by focusing on the positive and approaching life with a sense of hope and optimism, we can live our lives to the fullest and achieve our greatest potential.

31: Embracing Diversity and Inclusion

Introduction:

In a world where differences can often lead to division and conflict, embracing diversity and inclusion can help us to foster a more harmonious and inclusive society. The ability to recognize, appreciate, and celebrate differences can help us to build stronger relationships and create a more positive and supportive environment. In this chapter, we will explore the importance of embracing diversity and inclusion and how it can transform our lives and bring more positive energy into our world.

The Importance of Diversity and Inclusion:

Diversity and inclusion are two of the most important elements of a thriving and successful community. They help us to understand and appreciate the unique experiences, perspectives, and cultures that make up our world. They allow us to embrace our differences and create a more inclusive and supportive environment for everyone.

When we embrace diversity and inclusion, we are able to

bring together people from all walks of life and create a more vibrant and dynamic community. We are able to build stronger relationships and foster a deeper sense of understanding and respect for one another. This can lead to a more positive and supportive environment, where everyone feels valued and included.

The Benefits of Embracing Diversity and Inclusion:

There are numerous benefits to embracing diversity and inclusion, including increased creativity and innovation, improved decision-making, and a more harmonious and supportive community. By embracing diversity, we are able to tap into a wider range of perspectives, experiences, and skills, which can lead to more creative and innovative solutions to problems.

In addition, when we embrace diversity and inclusion, we are able to make more informed decisions, as we are able to consider a wider range of perspectives and opinions. This can help us to make better decisions and create a more equitable and just society.

Finally, by embracing diversity and inclusion, we are able to create a more harmonious and supportive community.

31: EMBRACING DIVERSITY AND INCLUSION

When we value and appreciate differences, we are able to build stronger relationships and create a more positive and inclusive environment for everyone.

How to Embrace Diversity and Inclusion:

Embracing diversity and inclusion requires a commitment to understanding and appreciating differences, as well as a willingness to challenge our own biases and assumptions. Here are some tips for embracing diversity and inclusion:

– Educate yourself about different cultures and perspectives: Take the time to learn about different cultures and perspectives, and be open to new ideas and experiences. This will help you to broaden your understanding and appreciation of diversity.

– Be an active listener: When engaging with people from different backgrounds, be an active listener and take the time to truly understand their perspectives and experiences. This will help you to build stronger relationships and foster a deeper sense of understanding and respect.

– Challenge your biases and assumptions: Take a close look at your own biases and assumptions, and work to challenge and overcome them. This will help you to create a more inclusive and supportive environment.

– Practice empathy: Put yourself in someone else's shoes and try to understand their experiences and perspectives. This will help you to build stronger relationships and create a more positive and supportive environment.

– Get involved in diversity and inclusion initiatives: Seek out opportunities to get involved in diversity and inclusion initiatives in your community, such as volunteering for a cultural festival or participating in a diversity training program.

Conclusion:

Embracing diversity and inclusion is an essential part of creating a positive and supportive environment for everyone. By understanding and appreciating differences, we are able to build stronger relationships and foster a deeper sense of understanding and respect for one another. Whether it is through education, active listening, challenging our own biases and assumptions, practicing empathy, or getting involved in

32: Building Strong Self-Esteem

Self-esteem is the foundation of our well-being and happiness, as it determines how we perceive and value ourselves. A strong self-esteem allows us to approach life with confidence and resilience, while a low self-esteem can lead to negative thoughts and emotions, hindering our progress and happiness. In this chapter, we will explore the importance of building strong self-esteem and the strategies you can use to develop a positive self-image.

The Importance of Self-Esteem

Self-esteem is a crucial aspect of our lives that influences many areas, including our relationships, career, and overall happiness. When we have high self-esteem, we have a positive outlook on life and are able to approach challenges with confidence. On the other hand, low self-esteem can result in negative self-talk, anxiety, and a lack of motivation, which can impact our overall well-being.

How to Build Strong Self-Esteem

Building strong self-esteem takes time and effort, but it is an achievable goal. Here are a few strategies you can use to develop a positive self-image:

– Practice self-compassion - Start by being kind and gentle with yourself. Treat yourself with the same compassion and understanding that you would offer to a good friend.

– Celebrate your accomplishments - Recognize your successes, no matter how small, and take time to celebrate them. This will help you see the positive aspects of yourself and build your confidence.

– Surround yourself with positive influences - Seek out friends, family, and other individuals who support and encourage you. Surrounding yourself with positive influences can help you build your self-esteem and improve your overall outlook on life.

– Focus on your strengths - Instead of dwelling on your weaknesses, focus on your strengths and the things you excel at. This will help you feel good about yourself and increase your confidence.

– Challenge negative self-talk - When negative thoughts arise, challenge them by reframing them into positive affirmations. Repeat these affirmations to yourself daily to help shift your focus from negative self-talk to positive self-talk.

32: BUILDING STRONG SELF-ESTEEM

The Benefits of Strong Self-Esteem

Having strong self-esteem has numerous benefits, including:

− Improved relationships - When you have high self-esteem, you are more likely to have healthy, fulfilling relationships. You are also less likely to tolerate unhealthy or toxic relationships, as you have a strong sense of self-worth.

− Increased resilience - People with high self-esteem are able to bounce back from challenges and setbacks more easily. They are less likely to be impacted by negative experiences, as they have a positive outlook and belief in themselves.

− Increased motivation - When you have a positive self-image, you are more likely to take action and pursue your goals. You have a greater sense of self-efficacy, which can drive you to achieve your dreams.

− Improved overall well-being - Strong self-esteem has a positive impact on our overall well-being, as it allows us to approach life with confidence and a positive outlook. This can lead to greater happiness, fulfillment, and satisfaction.

In conclusion, building strong self-esteem is an important aspect of personal growth and happiness. By following the strategies outlined in this chapter, you can develop a positive self-image and unlock your full potential. Remember, it takes time and effort to build strong self-esteem, but the benefits are well worth it. So, be patient and kind to yourself, and continue to work on developing a positive self-image. With time and dedication, you

33: The Importance of Self-Care

Self-care is an essential aspect of life that is often over-looked or neglected. Many people are so focused on achieving success, reaching their goals, and caring for others that they forget to take care of themselves. However, the reality is that without self-care, it is impossible to have the energy and vitality required to achieve our dreams and goals. That is why it is so important to make self-care a priority and understand its true benefits.

Self-care refers to activities and practices that help to maintain and improve our physical, emotional, and mental well-being. It can include anything from getting enough sleep, eating a balanced diet, exercising regularly, to engaging in leisure activities and hobbies. Self-care is not selfish, it is necessary for our health and overall happiness.

There are many benefits of self-care, some of which include:

– Increased Energy and Vitality

Self-care helps to keep our bodies and minds healthy and functioning at their best. Regular exercise and a healthy diet can boost our energy levels and give us the vitality we need to tackle the challenges of daily life.

33: THE IMPORTANCE OF SELF-CARE

– Improved Mental Health

Self-care is also critical for our mental health. Regular activities such as meditation, mindfulness, and journaling can help us to manage stress, reduce anxiety, and improve our mood.

– Better Relationships

When we take care of ourselves, we are able to show up in our relationships in a more positive and loving way. We are better able to communicate, listen, and be present for others when we have taken the time to care for ourselves.

– Increased Self-Awareness

Self-care activities can also help us to become more self-aware. By engaging in activities that promote self-reflection, we can gain a deeper understanding of our thoughts, feelings, and motivations, which can help us to make positive changes in our lives.

– Improved Resilience

Self-care helps to build resilience, which is our ability to bounce back from stress and adversity. When we take care of ourselves, we are better equipped to handle life's challenges and setbacks.

In conclusion, self-care is a critical aspect of life that should not be overlooked or neglected. It is essential for our physical, emotional, and mental well-being, and has many benefits that can help us to achieve our goals and live our best life. So, make sure to prioritize self-care and incorporate activities and practices that promote your well-being into your daily routine. Remember, self-care is not selfish, it is necessary for your health and happiness.

34: Living in the Moment: A Day-to-Day Guide

The key to unlocking your full potential and experiencing true happiness and fulfillment is to live in the present moment. In this chapter, we will explore the practical steps you can take each day to cultivate a more mindful and intentional approach to life, so that you can make the most of every moment.

Step 1: Start the day with gratitude

Begin each day by focusing on what you are grateful for. Take a moment to reflect on the things in your life that bring you joy and fulfillment, and express your gratitude for them. This could be as simple as listing three things you are thankful for each morning or writing a quick note in your journal. Starting the day with a positive and thankful mindset sets the tone for the rest of your day and helps you maintain a positive outlook.

Step 2: Practice mindfulness

Mindfulness is a powerful tool that can help you stay present and focused on the moment. Try to incorporate mindfulness practices into your daily routine, such as deep breathing exercises, meditating, or simply taking a few minutes each day to focus on your breath and your surroundings. This can help you cultivate a greater awareness of your thoughts and emotions, so that you can respond to them with compassion and understanding.

Step 3: Prioritize self-care

Self-care is an essential component of living in the moment. Take time each day to engage in activities that nourish your body, mind, and spirit, such as exercising, reading a book, or simply taking a relaxing bath. By taking care of yourself, you create a foundation of physical, emotional, and mental well-being that enables you to better manage the stress and challenges of daily life.

Step 4: Connect with others

Humans are social creatures, and connection with others is an important part of our happiness and well-being. Take time each day to connect with the people in your life, whether that's through phone calls, text messages, or in-person visits. Building strong, supportive relationships helps us feel connected and supported, and provides us with a sense of community and belonging.

Step 5: Engage in meaningful activities

By engaging in activities that bring you joy and fulfillment, you tap into the power of positive energy and flow. Whether it's volunteering, pursuing a passion, or simply spending time with loved ones, find ways to bring meaning and purpose into your life each day. When you are doing what you love, time seems to fly by, and you feel fully engaged and alive.

By following these simple steps, you can cultivate a more mindful and intentional approach to life and unlock the full potential of the present moment. Whether you are looking to transform your life, build stronger relationships, or simply experience more happiness and joy, the key to success lies in living in the moment. So embrace each day with open arms, and allow the power of positive energy to guide you on your journey towards a more fulfilling and meaningful life.

35: Achieving Flow: The Path Forward

In this final chapter of our book, "Flow: Transform Your Life with the Power of Positive Energy", we will discuss the path forward in achieving flow, the ultimate goal of all the principles and practices we have covered thus far. Flow is a state of mind where you are fully engaged in the present moment and experience a sense of effortless, positive energy. When you are in flow, you are at your most creative, productive, and fulfilled.

To achieve flow, you must first understand the principles of positive energy and be mindful of the present moment. You must also have a clear sense of purpose and be able to set meaningful goals for yourself. Additionally, you must have the resilience to overcome obstacles and embrace change, as well as the confidence to take risks and pursue your passions.

The first step in achieving flow is to cultivate positive energy in your daily life. This can be done by focusing on your thoughts and emotions, and by surrounding yourself with positive people and experiences. You can also practice self-care and engage in activities that bring you joy and peace.

Next, you must set goals for yourself and work towards them with purpose and dedication. This will require you to be organized and disciplined, and to prioritize your time effectively. You can also use visualization techniques, such as creating a vision board, to help you stay focused on your goals.

To build resilience, you must learn to embrace change and uncertainty, and to view challenges as opportunities for growth and learning. You can also develop a strong support system, and seek out resources and support when you need it.

To build confidence, you must learn to trust in your abilities and to take risks. You can also seek out new experiences and opportunities for personal growth, and practice self-affirmations and positive self-talk.

Finally, to truly live in the moment and experience flow, you must be mindful and intentional in your daily life. This means slowing down and taking time to appreciate the present moment, and to focus on your thoughts, emotions, and sensations. You can also engage in mindfulness practices, such as meditation or yoga, to help you cultivate mindfulness and live in the moment.

In conclusion, achieving flow is a journey that requires a combination of positive energy, purpose, resilience, confidence, and mindfulness. By following the principles and practices outlined in this book, you can transform your life and unlock your full potential with the power of positive energy. So take a deep breath, embrace the journey, and let the flow begin!

36: Conclusion: Embracing the Power of Positive Energy and Living in the Moment

In this book, we have explored the principles of flow and how they can transform your life with the power of positive energy. We have discussed the importance of finding your passion and purpose, setting goals, creating a vision board, overcoming procrastination, developing resilience, embracing change, finding balance in life, dealing with stress, building confidence, volunteering and giving back, the power of positive thinking, embracing diversity and inclusion, building strong self-esteem, the importance of self-care, and how to live in the moment on a day-to-day basis.

By embracing the principles of flow and the power of positive energy, you can unlock your full potential and live a more fulfilling and meaningful life. The key to success lies in embracing change, building resilience, and living in the moment. By staying present and focusing on the present moment, you can cultivate a positive attitude, build self-esteem, and increase your overall well-being.

In conclusion, the path forward to achieving flow in your

36: CONCLUSION: EMBRACING THE POWER OF POSIT-IVE ENERGY AND LIVING IN THE MOMENT

life is through embracing the power of positive energy, living in the moment, and pursuing your passions with purpose. Whether you are just starting out on your journey or have been working on your personal development for some time, remember that every small step counts, and that you are capable of making a positive impact in your own life and in the lives of others.

So, take a deep breath, embrace the power of positive energy, and start living in the moment. The future is yours to create, and with the principles of flow as your guide, you can transform your life and unlock your full potential.

Thank You

As we reach the end of this book, I want to say thanks for reading this book.

I want to get this information out to as many people as possible. If you found this book helpful, I would greatly appreciate you leaving me a review. This helps others find the book as well.

Disclaimer

This document is geared towards providing exact and reliable information in regards to the topic and issue covered. The publication is sold on the idea that the publisher is not required to render an accounting, officially permitted, or otherwise, qualified services. If advice is necessary, legal, financial, medical or professional, a practiced individual in the profession should be ordered.

This information is not presented by a financial or medical practitioner and is for entertainment, educational and informational purposes only. The content is not intended as a substitute for professional medical advice, diagnosis, or treatment. Always seek the advice of your physician or other qualified health care provider with any questions you may have regarding a medical condition. Never disregard professional medical advice or delay in seeking it because of something you have read.

The information provided herein is stated to be truthful and consistent, in that any liability, in terms of inattention or otherwise, by any usage or abuse of any policies, processes, or directions contained within is the solitary and utter responsibility of the recipient reader. Under no circumstances

DISCLAIMER

will any legal responsibility or blame be held against the publisher for any reparation, damages, or monetary loss due to the information herein, either directly or indirectly.